the
ART *of*
FASHION
JOURNAL

INSPIRATIONS TO
HELP YOU ACHIEVE
YOUR MOST
STYLISH LIFE

BY EILA MELL

Bluestreak
BOOKS

⩮Bluestreak

an imprint of Weldon Owen
Weldon Owen is a division of Bonnier Publishing USA
1045 Sansome Street, San Francisco, CA 94111
www.weldonowen.com

© 2017 Weldon Owen, Inc.

Written and edited by Eila Mell
Cover and Interior design by Amanda Richmond
Cover illustration and illustrations on pages 26, 46, 56,
78, 95, 122, 132, 142, and 152 by Tracy Turnbull
Illustrations on pages 6 and 16 from Shutterstock
All other art by Tabi Zarrinnaal

Library of Congress Cataloging in Publication data is available.

ISBN 978-1-6818-8196-6

First Printed in 2017
10 9 8 7 6 5 4 3 2 1

Printed in China by 1010 Printing

Contents

INTRODUCTION

Oscar de la Renta, Cristobal Balenciaga, Yves Saint Laurent, Christian Dior, Marc Jacobs, Coco Chanel, Alexander McQueen.

This is just a small sample of fashion designers whose work has changed the way we think about fashion, as well as the way we dress. Take the little black dress, a term that is so iconic that many of us simply refer to it as an LBD. In 1926 Coco Chanel designed a simple black crepe de Chine sheath with long narrow sleeves (accessorized with a string of white pearls). *Vogue* correctly predicted women would adopt this look in favor of the fussier, more elaborate styles that had dominated women's closets up to then. Almost 100 years later, the LBD is still a wardrobe staple.

In 1947 Christian Dior showed his first collection which included the innovative Bar Suit. The suit's style elements included full skirts, tiny waists, a mid calf-length, soft shoulders, and emphasized a sexy bust. Carmel Snow, the Editor-in-Chief of *Harper's Bazaar,* told Dior his dresses had such a 'new look.' With that, the collection was forever known as Dior's New Look and ushered in an era of ultra feminine fashion that would resonate for years to come.

We deal with fashion every time we open our closets to get dressed. Some of us love putting together a look that tells the world who we are, while others are more practical with their daily choices. Either way (and whether we think about it or not), we all have a personal style. This journal is a tool for perfecting your best style. Inside the pages you'll find tips and quotes that will guide you in nailing your best looks for every occasion. In addition to beautiful illustrations, you'll find plenty of room for writing, sketching, or jotting down any inspiration that strikes.

There is an It Girl (or Boy) in all of us. The key elements to finding yours are all here.

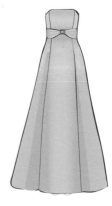

LIFE IS
TOO SHORT
TO WEAR
BORING
CLOTHES

YOUR CLOSET

A well-organized closet is the key to dressing your best every day. How can you look fantastic if you can't find what you're looking for? If you hang items by category (tops, pants, etc.) you can easily grab what you need.

Get a tape measure and take your measurements.

This is an invaluable tool, especially when shopping online.

SHOULDERS: Measure from the top of one shoulder all around your body

BUST: Measure around the fullest part of your bust

WAIST: Measure the smallest part of your waist (just above the navel)

HIPS: Measure just below the hip bone, making sure the tape measure wraps around the widest part of your rear

When hanging tops, it's very helpful to group same sleeve lengths together. For example, start with sleeveless, than gradually get longer. Short sleeves, mid-length, long sleeves.

How to
Determine
Your Body Type

Knowing your body type can help
you make great wardrobe choices.

~~~~~

INVERTED TRIANGLE
Shoulder or bust larger than hips

GOOD CHOICES:
bright bottoms, wide-leg pants, full skirts,
high waists, accentuated waistlines

~~~~~

RECTANGLE
Shoulders, bust, and hips are similar
size, no defined waistline

GOOD CHOICES:
scoop necks, long jackets, layers,
colorful bottoms, tops with ruffles

TRIANGLE (PEAR)

Hips wider than shoulders

GOOD CHOICES:

A-line skirts, light tops with dark bottoms,
boat neck tops, strapless dresses

~~~~~~~~~

HOURGLASS

Shoulders and hips similar size,
defined waistline

GOOD CHOICES:

fitted dresses, belts, wrap dresses,
high waisted skirts, skinny or
straight leg jeans

~~~~~~~~~

APPLE

Torso and upper body wider
than hips, no defined waistline

GOOD CHOICES:

monochromatic looks, V-necks,
empire tops and dresses,
flared or boot cut jeans

Fabric Tutorial

Chambray

A cotton material resembling light weight denim.

Eyelet

A sweet pattern of cutouts and embroidery.

Mesh

A netlike breathable fabric.

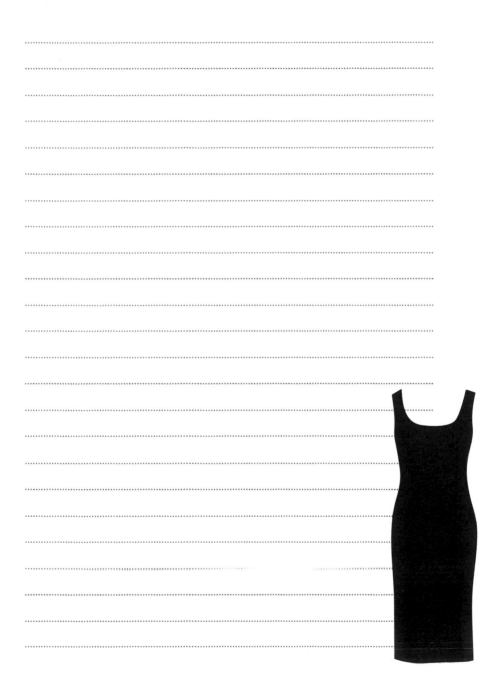

THE SPACE IN YOUR CLOSET IS VALUABLE.

It's better to have extra room than to keep something you never wear because you might need it at some point.

~~~~~~~~

YOUR CLOSET IS NO PLACE FOR NOSTALGIA.

If you're keeping something purely for nostalgia either put it in storage or take a picture of it and donate it to charity. The picture will evoke the same memory and take up much less space.

SHOPPING

Think about the fitting room before you get dressed to go shopping. It's so much easier to take a pullover on and off while trying things on than to keep buttoning and unbuttoning all day long.

Sit down when trying on pants. If the zipper pulls or bunches try a different size.

Fabric Tutorial

Linen

A natural, breathable fabric made from flax.

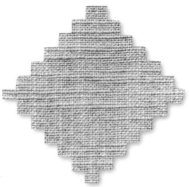

Tartan

A Scottish pattern of crisscrossing colors.

Brocade

Heavy fabric with a subtle sheen.

....

....

....

....

....

....

....

....

....

....

....

....

....

....

....

....

....

....

....

The layouts of stores are designed to encourage us to spend money. Be aware that carpet can be used strategically to slow shoppers down (this is especially true for women with strollers). Higher priced items are usually found in these areas.

*"Fashion is the armor
to survive the reality
of everyday life."*

—BILL CUNNINGHAM

Knowing what's in your closet is the first step to having your best wardrobe.

Make a list of how many pants, tops, skirts, etc., that you have. When you go shopping you'll be much less likely to buy something similar.

PANTS

....

....

....

....

....

....

....

SHIRTS

....

....

....

....

....

....

....

....

SKIRTS

....

....

....

....

....

....

SWEATERS

....

....

....

....

....

....

DRESSES

....

....

....

....

....

Sizes vary from designer to designer.

Write down the size you wear in each designer, and you'll save loads of time shopping. Include shoes too!

DESIGNER	SHIRT SIZE	PANTS SIZE	DRESS SIZE	SHOE SIZE

*"Whoever said that money
can't buy happiness, simply didn't
know where to go shopping."*

-BO DEREK

INSPIRATION

Use photos of looks you like on other people
to inspire, but never copy an outfit head to toe.
Take the look and adapt it to your style
and what you have in your closet.

Fabric Tutorial

Gingham

A two color woven check pattern.

Cotton Gauze

Loosely woven, delicate fibers often have a deliberately crinkled look.

Chevron

A multicolored pattern of converging V's on a loose, textural knit.

Trends can be a great source for inspiration,

but never follow them blindly. If saddlebags are an issue for you, bypass skinny jeans whether they're all the rage or not. When a trend works for your body type, that's the time to go all in.

Let your own wardrobe inspire you.
Throw a skirt over a dress and wear it in
a whole new way. Mix up your suits and pair
with different items. If it doesn't work, what's
the harm? Take it off and try something
else. Have fun getting dressed!

INSPIRATION BOARD

Sketch or attach pictures that
inspire your personal style.

UNDER YOUR CLOTHES

A bra that's too small can make a woman look like she has four boobs. This is not cute. Ever.

Bra Guide

SOFT CUP

No underwire. Best for small busts.

ADHESIVE

A stick-on bra. Ideal for backless dresses and tops.

PUSH-UP

Lifts, separates and pads. Good for low-cut tops.

FULL-COVERAGE

Contoured cups and no-show seams. Great for large busts.

BALCONETTE

Half-cup style that frames and boosts.

DEMI

A thin, slight bra that cuts straight across the bust.

LONGLINE

Provides support and smooths the stomach.

FRONT CLOSURE

Clasp in the front.

BULLET

Pointed cone shape made famous by Madonna and Jean-Paul Gaultier.

CAMISOLE

A lace or satin overlay creates the look of a camisole.

BANDEAU

A tube made of stretchy fabric. Best for small busts.

bra
basics

STRAPS

These adjustable elasticized straps should fit snugly but smoothly against your flesh, and not dig or leave red marks. Bras get looser over time; if you have to adjust these too much at your first fitting, the band is probably too big—and will only get bigger

CUPS

Look out for overflow on the top or sides, or a center tab that refuses to lie flat against your skin—signs that a bra is too small. If there's excess room in the cups, go down a size—likewise if there are wrinkles across the cups or the center tab puckers.

UNDERWIRE

This thin little line of wire sure can poke and prod, so move your arms up and down to make sure it doesn't gouge at the sides or in the center of the bust when you move.

BAND

When trying on a bra, look to make sure the band is horizontal. A band that rides up can cause unsightly bulges. You should be able to fit two fingers underneath the band in the back, and one in the front.

"Playing dress-up begins at age five and never truly ends."

—KATE SPADE

OWN BRAS WITH A VARIETY OF STRAP STYLES;

that way you're never left with exposed lingerie. Or choose a convertible bra, which lets you make your own configurations.

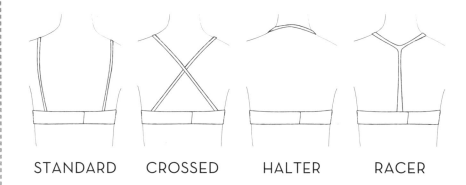

STANDARD   CROSSED   HALTER   RACER

SHAPEWEAR is not only for people who want to appear slimmer. That is a fantastic feature to be sure, but not the only benefit. It's the easiest way to get a smooth line under your clothing. You'll never have VPL (visible panty line) with shapewear. It Is also your best defense against unwanted lumps and bumps. 99% of celebrities are wearing it on the red carpet, and you can too.

A nude bra is more invisible under a white top than a white bra.

‌

‌

‌

‌

‌

‌

‌

‌

‌

‌

‌

‌

‌

‌

‌

‌

‌

‌

‌

‌

Too many women expect their bra straps to do the heavy lifting, but it's the band that should be your bra's main source of support. If the band rides up in the back you need a smaller (band) size. If your straps dig into your shoulders your band is most likely also too loose. If they're too loose try a larger size.

TOPS

Make sure your button down shirts fit
properly across your chest. You don't want
to be at a business meeting with your bra
peeking through a gap when viewed from the
side. A good way to avoid this is to stretch
your arms back, widening your chest.
If your shirt gaps it's not the right fit.

tops
defined

CREW NECK
A circular neckline that fits snug around the base of the neck. Plays up small chests.

POLO
The short, pointed collar creates a mix of sporty and preppy, and can make you look taller.

SPLIT NECK
An enticing slice draws eyes down and makes the neck look longer. A tamer v-neck.

SHELL
The most basic of sleeveless tops. For a trim shape, seek armholes that cut in on the shoulder.

CAMISOLE
A graceful tank alternative and a layering must-have. The wide neck flatters most physiques.

V-NECK
Hot on everyone. A wide neckline balances out bottom curves; a narrow one is slimming.

HENLEY
A collarless cousin of the polo, but with playful buttons that let you adjust for a fit that flatters.

BOAT NECK
A neckline that runs from shoulder to shoulder. Long torsos benefit from the horizontal line.

SCOOP NECK TANK
The round dip elongates necks, balances oval faces, and minimizes curves. Magical!

A v-neck is flattering on all body types, so it's never a bad idea to buy one you love.

If you want to play up a small bust, an embellished top is a great way to go. Conversely, if you want to downplay a large chest, stay away from shine or adornment.

shirt
basics

COLLAR
Look for collar types that balance your face shape, rather than those that mirror and exaggerate your face's dimensions. If you have delicate features, choose a small collar that won't overpower them.

SLEEVE
A narrow sleeve with a small armhole suits most—it cuts down on baggy excess fabric. The seam connecting sleeve to shirt should glide across the edge of your shoulder.

BODY
A flattering shirt fits closely enough that it doesn't balloon when tucked in, but it shouldn't be so snug that it tugs at the shoulder seams or the placket (the opening where button meets buttonhole).

BUST
When trying on a shirt, button it all the way up—the placket should lay flat along the bust. To flatter a fuller chest, choose a shirt with darts; to play up a smaller one, look for pockets and details like ruffles or gathers.

LENGTH
For most, the bottom hem should hit 2 inches (5 cm) below the waist. Shirts that hit where the hips begin to flare flatter bottom curves; small derrieres look great in shirts that hit halfway down the backside.

sleeve
lengths

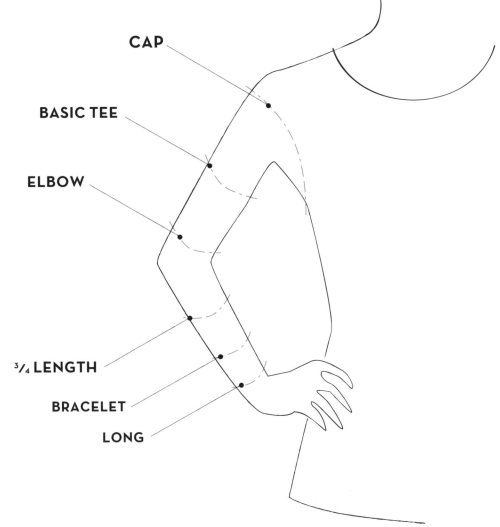

CAP

BASIC TEE

ELBOW

³/₄ LENGTH

BRACELET

LONG

Test your shirt knowledge!

1. WHAT TYPE OF SHIRT IS A TAILORED CLASSIC?
   a. Jabot
   b. Oxford
   c. Wrap

2. WHICH TOP HAS A PETER PAN COLLAR?

a.    **b**.    **c**.

3. A SWEETHEART NECK IS:
   a. A high, rounded neckline
   b. A heart-shaped neckline
   c. Wide with rounded lapels

Answers: **1.** b   **2.** c **3.** b

INSPIRATION BOARD

Sketch or attach pictures that
inspire your personal style.

PANTS

Pants with a slight flare are slimming
on just about all body types.

Pockets

CARGO

IN-SEAM

 SLASH

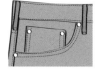 COIN

ROUNDED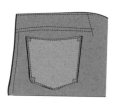

PATCH  FLAP

WELT   ZIP

Can you ID these pants styles?

1. TROUSER

a.

b.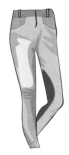

c.

2. PALAZZO

a.

b.

c.

BALLOON

a.

b.

c.

ANSWERS: 1. c **2.** a **3.** c

a guide to jeans

1. CARPENTER
Workwear-inspired details like hammer loops and utility pockets.

2. HIGH-WAISTED
Jeans with a high waist.

3. SKINNY
Snug fit.

4. STRAIGHT
Classic fit with a straight leg.

5. WIDE LEG
Flares from the hips.

6. FLARED
Narrow to the knee, then flares.

7. TROUSER
Slash pockets, extended tab and a front crease.

8. MOTO
Motorcycle gear inspired with extra seams around the knees.

9. BOYFRIEND
Roomy, straight fit.

10. BOOT CUT
Slight flare from the knee to fit over boots.

11. BELL BOTTOM
Fitted through the thigh with extra flare from the knee.

Waistbands

TAB   EXTENDED TAB   SIDE ZIP   FOLDOVER

TIE   DRAWSTRING   ELASTIC

JEANS ARE MORE DIFFICULT TO SHOP FOR THAN OTHER PANTS.
Be prepared to spend some time trying on many different shapes and styles.

pants basics

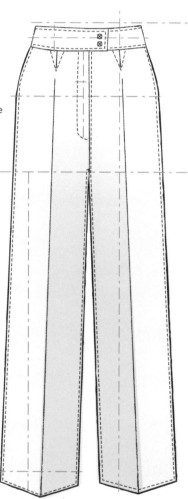

WAISTBAND

A low rise may be sexy, but look out for bulges over the band. Pants that hit at the natural waist can conceal a tummy, while high rises hit closer to the navel and make legs look long. Be careful with excess fabric between the crotch and waistband, which can make legs look shorter.

SIDE POCKETS

Slash and in-seam pockets can flatter (especially those who want to look a little curvier), but they can also gape and add bulk in the wrong places. If that's the case, pick pants with pockets that lie flat, or have them sewn shut.

SEAT

Don't be shy about wearing pants that snugly skim your bottom, but watch for wrinkles along the thigh or at the outer seams. To play up your backside, go for detailed yokes and embroidery; to downplay it, opt for large pockets midway up the seat.

LENGTH

For a long line, the hem should hit about 1 inch (2.5 cm) from the floor when you're in heels. (If you have a go-to pair, bring them to your fitting.) When in flats, the hem should brush the tops of your shoes.

LEG

You can't go wrong with a pant that's fitted through the hip and flares out gently from the knee, a shape that creates a svelte line on almost anyone. Cropped styles can be just right on petite women, while straight-leg or boot-cut pants flatter voluptuous figures.

The best way to balance pants with
a wide leg is with a fitted top.

Pant
Lengths

HOT PANTS ....

SHORT SHORTS ....

MIDTHIGH ....

BERMUDA ....

PEDAL PUSHER ....

GAUCHO ....

CAPRI ....

ANKLE ....

CLASSIC ....

SKIRTS

An A-line skirt will give the
appearance of a smaller waist.

A skirt that fits properly won't ride up when you walk.

....

....

....

....

....

....

....

....

....

....

....

....

....

....

....

....

....

....

....

....

....

....

skirt
lengths

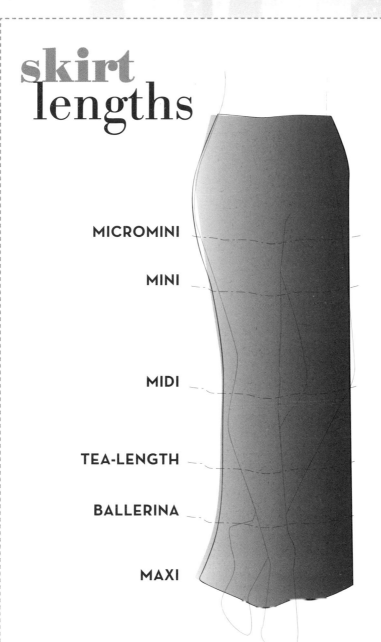

MICROMINI

MINI

MIDI

TEA-LENGTH

BALLERINA

MAXI

**Miniskirts work especially
well with flats.**

Skirt styles that always work

PENCIL

A-LINE

CIRCLE

skirt basics

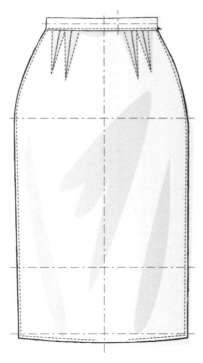

WAIST

A skirt that comes up to your natural waist lets fabric drape gracefully around your torso without creating bulges. To tuck a tummy, choose a skirt without a waistband or with a side zipper. To amp up your curve factor or add volume, go for pleats, gathers, or wide waistbands.

BODY

Slim A-line shapes are a sure bet for concealing bottom-half concerns—but beware of a skirt that's too full, as it can add pouf where you don't want it. Straight skirts lengthen the body and are perfect on petites. You can boost curves with a skirt that tapers toward the hem.

REAR

You'll want the back of the skirt to tautly skim the body line without tightness, rippling seams, or bunching fabric. A lining can help achieve a smooth, even fit.

LENGTH

A flattering skirt will hit at one of the narrowest parts of the leg—for most women, that means midthigh or just above or below the knee. Once you find your best length, you can get almost any skirt adjusted by a tailor to be just so.

"*I don't design clothes.*
I design dreams."

—RALPH LAUREN

INSPIRATION BOARD

Sketch or attach pictures that
inspire your personal style.

DRESSES

If you have limited time to put a look together, a dress is the answer. All you need to worry about is pairing it with a great pair of shoes, and you're ready to go!

A wrap dress is great for curvy shapes, as it accentuates the waist while slimming the body. If your wrap dress is too low cut, a camisole peeking through underneath is a great addition.

A great way to wear sleeveless dresses in the winter is to pair them with a turtleneck underneath.

dress
basics

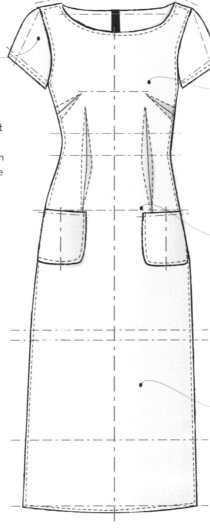

ARMHOLES

For dresses that are fitted or sewn from thicker fabrics, lift and lower your arms while standing and then sitting. There should be breathing room under the arm—no gapping, pulling, or digging. For less structured frocks, check that your bra doesn't peek out from under the armhole.

BODY

A semifitted dress that shows the waist flatters almost everyone, but watch for horizontal wrinkles that mean it's a bit snug. Straight shapes are best on narrow figures, while volume above or below the waist helps balance out curves.

BUST

Whether a drapey or fitted bodice, look for a bustline that shows your figure without flattening or bagginess. If you go up a size, a tailor can customize the fit to get it just right.

WAIST

An empire waist can elongate the legs, and low or dropped waists are best on narrow or short-waisted frames. Belting most dresses at the natural waist creates a nice line on both boyish and curvacious figures. To hide a tummy, belt it higher, or find a dress with vertical seams.

SKIRT

Examine the hemline from every angle—it should hang straight all the way around. If a dress doesn't fit properly, the skirt can bunch and pull when you move, so try sitting down and walking around. The hem or waist shouldn't ride up too much, and you should still feel comfortable, of course.

Fabric Tutorial

Silk Chiffon

A super thin, sheer and floaty fabric.

Batik

An African method of wax-resist dyeing uses natural colors and makes layered, exotic patterns.

Seersucker

A gently puckered fabric that's lightweight and usually features pastel stripes.

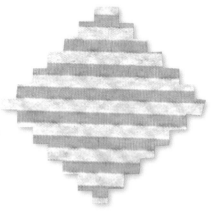

What style is this dress?

Answers: 1. Shift **2.** Caftan **3.** Sheath **4.** Shirt **5.** Slip
6. Sundress **7**. Ball Gown **8.** Mermaid **9.** Wrap **10.** Coat

INSPIRATION BOARD

Sketch or attach pictures that
inspire your personal style.

SHOES

A pointed toe will create the
illusion of a longer leg.

A wide heel is better than a thin one if you're going to be on your feet all day. Your weight will be distributed more evenly and you will be much more comfortable.

Shoes!

1. A ballet flat:
a. has a strap around the ankle
b. has a side tie
c. has a slim sole; usually with a tie at the toe

~~~~~~~~

2. A D'Orsay pump:
a. Reveals the arch and instep
b. Has a cutout heel
c. Is backless

~~~~~~~~

3. Espadrilles:
a. are typically a mix of canvas and straw
b. are made of clear plastic
c. have a tapered heel

Answers: **1.** c **2.** a **3.** a

Applying a clear gel deodorant can prevent your feet from getting blisters from shoes. Once the deodorant dries in the sensitive area it will create a barrier between your skin and stop the friction that causes blisters to occur.

Make a list of your shoes arranged by heel height.

It'll be helpful to see on paper to avoid buying similar shoes.

HIGH HEELS

....

....

....

MEDIUM HEELS

....

....

....

FLATS

....

....

....

SNEAKERS

....

....

....

BAGS

Keeping your essentials in a makeup case that goes in your bag makes it super simple to change your bag as often as you like. An added plus is that the lining is protected from the loss of a pen cap or lipstick top.

Where a bag sits on your body is important, as that feature will be accentuated. Bags that hit at the waist can give a nipped-in appearance and are ideal for most body shapes.

A colorful bag is the easiest way to
add punch to a neutral outfit.

10 Classic Bag Styles

SADDLE

HOBO

BAGUETTE

FRAME CLUTCH

CHAIN STRAP

MINAUDUERE

BUCKET

MESSENGER

SHOPPER

DOME

"Give a girl the right shoes
and she can conquer the world."

-MARILYN MONROE

....

....

....

....

....

....

....

....

....

....

....

....

....

....

....

....

....

....

....

....

....

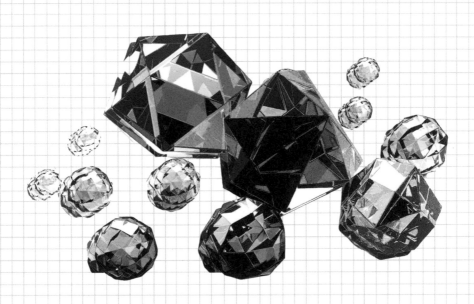

JEWELRY

A focal point is essential to showcasing your jewelry. If you're going with a statement necklace, keep the rest simple. Big earrings don't need to be paired with a necklace.

Earrings

STUD

CHANDELIER

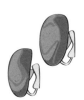

COSTUME

DANGLY

PLUG

WHIMSICAL

DROP

HOOP

GYPSY HOOP

BUTTON

GIRANDOLE

STACKED

SPIKE

PAVE

DISC

CUFF

PULL THROUGH

CAPTIVE BEAD

Bracelets

ID

LINK

WRAPAROUND

WIDE CUFF

ARM BAND

LACED

SAFETY PIN

BRAIDED

TENNIS

HINGED BANGLE

SPIKE

MULTISTRAND

CUFF

HAMMERED

GEOMETRIC

CELTIC

A brooch can easily become a necklace by stringing a chain through the clasp.

Pearls are a great alternative to diamonds, and are significantly less expensive.

Necklaces

ROPE

LAYERED

BIB

PENDANT

CLUSTER

SPACED BEAD

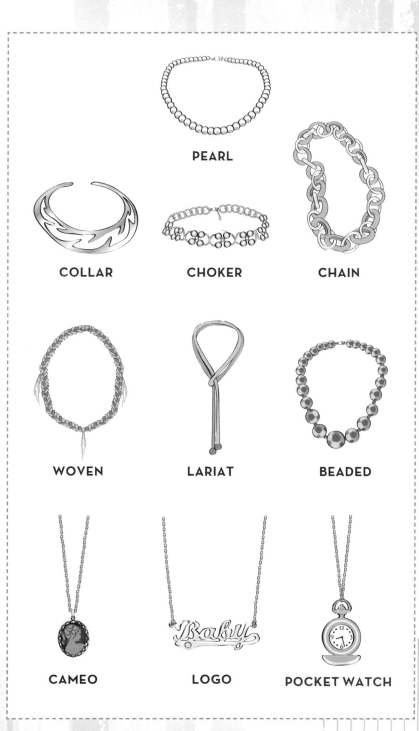

PEARL

COLLAR

CHOKER

CHAIN

WOVEN

LARIAT

BEADED

CAMEO

LOGO

POCKET WATCH

Rings

BOX

MOSAIC

BLOSSOM

SCATTER

DOME

CLUSTER

COIL

COCKTAIL

SCARAB

BAND

SOLITAIRE

CHANNEL

STACK

OVAL

KNUCKLE

DOUBLE KNUCKLE

SIGNET

CARTOUCHE

ARMOR

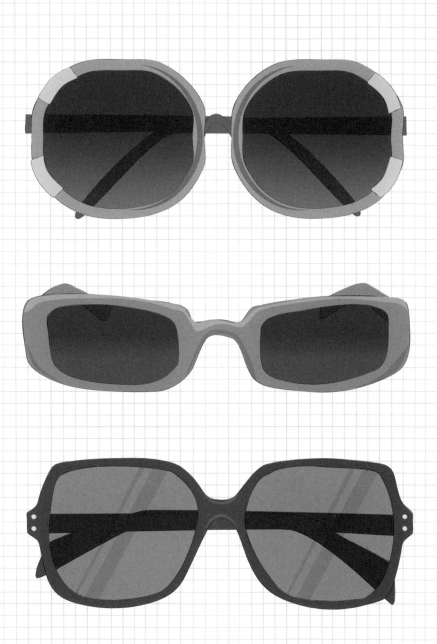

SUNGLASSES

Frames that contrast your face shape
will work best. Round frames work well
on heart-shaped faces, while aviators
are great for those with a square shape.

Oversize frames with a low bridge work well to camouflage a larger nose.

Sunglasses

AVIATOR

WAYFARER

OVERSIZE ROUND

CAT'S EYE

FLAT TOP

BUTTERFLY

It's not worth spending a lot on sunglasses if you lose them often.

....

....

....

....

....

....

....

....

....

....

....

....

....

....

....

....

....

....

....

....

....

The reason sunglasses can be expensive is the UVA and UVB protection that prevent sun damage, as well as polarized lenses that reduce the need for squinting.

OUTERWEAR

During the cold months there is no more
important piece in your wardrobe than your
coat. Spend as much as you can comfortably
afford to get the best coat you can find. After
all, you'll be seen in it more than any other item
in your closet for an entire season.

Down coats are warmer than any others. If you live anywhere that temperatures dip below 32 degrees, this matters.

Fabric Tutorial

Merino Wool

Merino sheep produce wool that's incredibly soft and warm, yet breathable.

Buffalo Plaid

A broad check, often white and black or red and black.

Fair Isle

A knitting technique that uses colorful yarn to produce vibrant and whimsical geometric patterns.

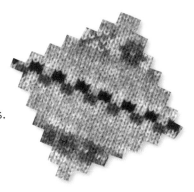

Make sure your coat has enough room so you can wear layers underneath.

Classic Coats

CAR
Collared coat that
hits midthigh.

CAMEL
Golden-brown coat
made of camel hair.

PARKA
Often has a fur-lined
hood and a long length

PEACOAT
Sailor-inspired
double-breasted with
wide, notched lapels.

TRENCH
Has a rain shield, gun flap
and D-ring belt.

MACINTOSH
Made of special plastic-coated
fabric to protect from the rain.

outerwear
basics

COLLAR

A V-shaped neckline with pointed lapels creates the leanest line— and the narrower the lapels, the longer you look. But you can rock any collar as long as it's not too fussy or exaggerated.

BUST

Those with fuller busts should steer clear of double-breasted styles or details like draping or embellishments on the placket—these are best for women who want to add more shape or volume. Everyone should look for a fit that doesn't gap or bulge.

BODY

For a perfectly proportional line, you'll want a coat to skim your body without being tighter in some areas than others. When you raise your arms, the fabric on the back shouldn't bunch up. If the slits in the back (called vents) are pulled open into a V-shape, the coat is too small.

SLEEVE

The hem should hit between the wrist and the thumb's bottom knuckle. Sleeves that cut in slightly will downplay wide shoulders.

LENGTH

Ladies on the petite side will look svelte in a coat that's knee-length or shorter, while tall women can sport longer coats and not overwhelm their figures. It may sound obvious, but consider your climate. If winters are ice-cold, go for a coat that's long or down-filled. In warmer regions, romp through the leaves in a cropped bomber.

INSPIRATION BOARD

Sketch or attach pictures that
inspire your personal style.

A NIGHT
ON THE TOWN

Have fun with your clothes.
A night on the town is the right time to
pull out your sparkles, sequins and fringe.

Obviously, we all want to look our
best on a date. To that end, the key is to wear whatever
you feel most confident in so you can relax and be yourself.
The last thing you want is to be adjusting a falling strap or
yanking down a too short skirt all night long.

Fabric Tutorial

Satin

Usually made from silk, satin has exquisite luster and drape.

Paisley

The swirling pattern of droplet shapes originated in India.

Toile

This French export features pastoral scenes, usually printed in just two colors.

Body skimming is a do. Skin tight is a don't.

"Your dresses should be tight enough to show you're a woman and loose enough to show you're a lady."

—EDITH HEAD

Make a list of your 10 favorite dresses.

Knowing what you love can help you avoid buying something you'll never wear. If all your favorites are solid colors, chances are that dress with the busy print that looked so good in the store will just hang in your closet.

1. ....

2. ....

3. ....

4. ....

5. ....

6. ....

7. ....

8. ....

9. ....

10. ....

INSPIRATION BOARD

Sketch or attach pictures that
inspire your personal style.

WORK ATTIRE

Too much exposed skin
is never okay for the office.

Business formal or boardroom attire
generally applies to high-level corporate or legal
professionals. This is not the time to show your funky side.
Conservative suits work best. Closed toe shoes are a must.

〰〰〰

Business professional is slightly more relaxed
than business formal. Conservative dressing is still
key, however you can get away with a bit more flair in your
accessories. Shoes still need to have closed toes.

Business casual is the most common dress
code in offices across the country. Separates instead
of suits are fine. Jewelry can be more ornate. Shoes
are more relaxed, but still should have closed toes.

~~~~~~~~

If you work in a creative field these rules
do not necessarily apply. Simply take your
cue from the boss and your co-workers.

Fabric Tutorial

Cashmere

Gathered from goats, it's the softest, finest wool.

Tweed

Heavyweight fabric woven from several colors of yarn.

Boucle

Woven from multiple strands of varying tautness. The looser threads make for a loopy, plush surface.

INSPIRATION BOARD

Sketch or attach pictures that
inspire your personal style.

SPECIAL OCCASION

Skip wearing white if you're
going to a wedding. You'll look like
you're trying to upstage the bride.

White tie is the most formal type of wedding.
Women are expected to wear a formal floor-length gown.

For a black tie wedding women can go with
a full-length gown, or opt for a formal cocktail-length dress.

Cocktail dresses or dressy separates are fine
for semi-formal or dressy casual weddings.
This also works if the invitation says festive attire.

A simple sundress is ideal for
a casual wedding or beach formal.

Fabric Tutorial

Pucci-inspired

A vibrant, swooshing pattern in kaleidoscope colors. First hit the scene with fashionistas in the '50s.

Silk Ombre

Vibrant colors fade into a dip-dyed gradient to make a dramatic impact.

Geometric

A bold, graphic pattern made up of artistic angles.

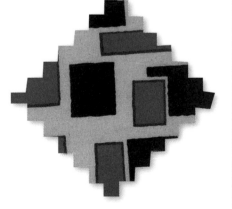

"One is never over-dressed or under-dressed with a Little Black Dress."

—KARL LAGERFELD

INSPIRATION BOARD

Sketch or attach pictures that
inspire your personal style.